SERENDIPITY SOLOS

Nine solo songs for young singers
by Lin Marsh

To buy Faber Music publications or to find out about the
full range of titles available please contact your local retailer
or Faber Music sales enquiries:

Faber Music Limited, Burnt Mill, Elizabeth Way, Harlow CM20 2HX England
Tel: +44 (0) 1279 82 89 82 Fax: +44 (0) 1279 82 89 83
sales@fabermusic.com fabermusic.com

FABER *ff* MUSIC

CONTENTS

Gr.2 B 1. The Cuckoo Clock .... page 3

2. My Shadow .... page 6

3. Little Old Lady .... page 8

Gr.3 B 4. Butterfly .... page 10

5. Dead Men and Gold .... page 12

6. The Fair .... page 14

7. Winter .... page 16

Gr.5 B 8. Windy Weather .... page 18

9. A King of Oaks .... page 20

The text paper used in this publication is a virgin fibre product
that is manufactured in the UK to ISO 14001 standards. The wood fibre used is only sourced
from managed forests using sustainable forestry principles. This paper is 100% recyclable.

© 2008 by Faber Music Ltd
3 Queen Square London WC1N 3AU
Cover by Lydia Merrills-Ashcroft
Music processed by MusicSet 2000
Printed in England by Caligraving Ltd
All rights reserved

ISBN 0-571-53240-3
EAN 978-0-571-53240-7

1. The Cuckoo Clock

Lin Marsh

As his lit - tle face peeps through. Call-ing ev - 'ry hour of the

night and day With a bright 'Cuck - oo! Cuck - oo!'

But what does he do all the rest of the day? Is he

hap - py on his own? Does he count ev - 'ry se - cond ev - 'ry

2. My Shadow

Lin Marsh

Who has chased me all the morn - ing?

Who has fol - low'd all the day? Who lies wait - ing

round the cor - ner just in case I run a - way?

Who lies lurk - ing in my bed - room, Tak - ing shape in eve - ning light? Danc - ing on my wall and ceil - ing As I lie in bed at night.

Who will rise with me to - mor - row Share my day from morn 'til eve? Ev - er faith - ful, ev - er watch - ful, Why, my sha - dow, I be - lieve!

3. Little Old Lady

Lin Marsh

stop and say 'Hel-lo'. Gone, the folk you used to greet.

3. Lit-tle old la - dy,

smil-ing at your mem - 'ries. Twi-light hour is fad - ing fast.

Safe in gen-tle slum - ber, as the long day clo - ses, Dream - ing of a

time long past.

4. Butterfly

Lin Marsh

5. Dead Men and Gold

Lin Marsh

1. Ten fa - thoms down ___ she lies in si - lence Lost in the o - cean's grave - yard deep.
2. Who kept the watch on this fate - ful voy - age? Who gave the or - ders as dark - ness fell?

Dead men and gold her sole com - pan - ions, Bur - ied a - live ___ in an end - less sleep.
Dead men and gold must keep their se - crets. Cen - tu - ries pass ___ yet ___ none may tell.

3. Where was she bound on that win-ter eve-ning? Who saw the signs of im-pend-ing doom? Dead men and gold know all the an-swers,

Slum-ber-ing on, slum-ber-ing on in their wa-t'ry tomb.

6. The Fair

Lin Marsh

1. Now the fair has come to town, ___ Watch the big wheel
2. Hus - tle bus - tle down the street, ___ Ev - 'ry-one's in
4. Co -lour'd lights on fan - cy stalls___ Beck - on ev - 'ry-

spin! ___ Bum - per cars and round - a - bouts, ___
town. ___ Ca - ra-vans and can - dy-floss, ___
where. ___ Hoops to spin and darts to throw ___

Co - co - nuts to win, ___
Laugh-ter all a - round. ___
Mu - sic in the air. ___

7. Winter

Lin Marsh

8. Windy Weather

Lin Marsh

Lyrics:

1. Oh for a day when the wind blows free And the wild, blue break-ers roar! _____ When the sea-gulls cry as they wheel and dive O'er the bare and rock-y shore. _____ And far out to sea in the

2. Oh for a day when the wind blows free and the air is fill'd with spray! _____ When the breeze it car-ries a taste of salt as it blows a-cross the bay. _____ For

2nd time to Coda

9. A King of Oaks

Lin Marsh

1. There stood in the for-est the migh-tiest of trees. A king of oaks was he. And proud-ly he reached till his arms touched the sky, His beau-ty for all to see.

2. For hun-dreds of years,—— through storm and through drought He brave-ly held his ground. And moved with the wind as it roared through his leaves, His cou-rage and strength re-

THE SONGSCAPE SERIES

LIN MARSH

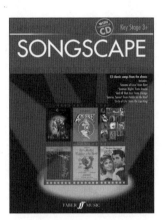

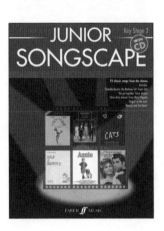

Key Stage 1–2	Key Stage 3
Junior Songscape (Book/CD) ISBN: 0-571-52077-4	Songscape (pupil's book) ISBN: 0-571-51866-4 10-pack: ISBN: 0-571-51944-X
Junior Songscape: Earth, Sea & Sky (Book/CD) ISBN: 0-571-52206-8	Songscape (teacher's book) ISBN: 0-571-51867-2
Junior Songscape: Stage & Screen (Book/CD) ISBN: 0-571-52503-2	Songscape: Stage & Screen (Book/ECD) ISBN: 0-571-52609-8
Junior Songscape: Children's Favourites (Book/2CDs) ISBN: 0-571-52644-6	Songscape: Christmas (Book/2CDs) ISBN: 0-571-52643-8

FABER *ff* MUSIC

To buy Faber Music publications or to find out about the full range of titles available
please contact your local music retailer or Faber Music sales enquiries:

Faber Music Ltd, Burnt Mill, Elizabeth Way, Harlow CM20 2HX
Tel: +44 (0) 1279 82 89 82   Fax: +44 (0) 1279 82 89 83
sales@fabermusic.com   fabermusic.com   expressprintmusic.com